Brian Swann
ROOTS

BRIAN SWANN

ROOTS

Photographs by Hardie Truesdale

NEW RIVERS PRESS 1976

CREDITS: "Faces" (under the title of "August Maine")
and "The Fly" appeared in YALE REVIEW; "Reaching"
in POETRY; "Cat Winter" in KANSAS QUARTERLY;
"A Hair of the Dog" in AN ANTHOLOGY OF YOUNGER
POETS (Ardis Press, 1976); "The Hand of the Hills" in
SALMAGUNDI; "A Dialog of Distances" (earlier form) in
MALAHAT REVIEW; "Floating" and "Northern Garland"
in ANTAEUS ("Northern Garland" also appeared in
MADEIRA & TOASTS FOR BASIL BUNTING'S 75TH
BIRTHDAY, Jargon Society, 1975; and "Year of the Bird"
in THE NATION. Our thanks to the editors of these pub-
lications for permission to reprint.

Our thanks also to the National Endowment for the Arts
and the New York State Council on the Arts for their
generosity and grant support.

New Rivers Press Books and Chapbooks are distributed by:
                    Serendipity Books
                    1790 Shattuck Avenue
                    Berkeley, California
                    94709

ROOTS has been manufactured in the United States of
America for New Rivers Press (C. W. Truesdale, editor/
publisher), P. O. Box 578, Cathedral Station, New York,
New York 10025 in a first edition of 750 copies of which
15 have been signed and numbered by the artists.

ROOTS

NORTHERN GARLAND

SURFACING

this is the last window

through the last window
a last dog
does last things

there is a cloud
that knows exactly where it is going
a bird freed of nests
a road surfacing

there is a room behind me labelled
Room
and a floor beneath labelled
Ceiling
the window stands alone
the walls have already left

I exit
leaving the window and its last things

I slip out the back
following my corner
to whichever landscape it might choose
to settle in

NORTHERN CROWN

for Kid Bacon & Mercury & SG

TRAILCLEARERS

we trace it anticlockwise
unwinding

it had assumed its own life

now under the machete the trail comes back
balsam pine aspen tamarack lopped
or torn from thin soil round the lake

there goes bill up ahead
swinging a swathe all round
keeping things open and i
not so keen
follow in white sneakers
with a folded saw smelling the resin
and trampled moss

bill gave that trail hell
& did all the work
till he asked me to saw a small spruce
which i did rapidly
and stood it up again
against a tamarack and in my head
heard Chief Little Crow:
"We are only a little herd of buffalo left scattered
The great herds that once covered the prairies
are no more
The white men are like locusts when they fly so thick
the whole sky is like a snowstorm
You may kill one two ten yes
as many as the leaves in the forest yonder
and their brothers will not miss them
Count your fingers all day long and white men with
guns in their hands will come faster than you can count

You are fools
You are like rabbits when the hungry wolves hunt them
in the hard moons
I am no coward
I will die with you"

and bill could have cut his leg off when
his machete glanced off a rock

we left nothing to chance even
slicing branches at the knife's extreme reach
over our heads
it would take some missing that trail

and when we had finished each side of the lake
communicated with each other
inside was our magic circle and outside darkness

back in the cabin no trail could be seen
but we knew it was out there

we knew that if we walked off right we would come back left
and vice versa

far off a pulp-truck rumbled a storm
and i remembered that when la salle
reached burnt out fort crèvecoeur
in his search for tonty
he found this on the planks of the unfinished boat:
"nous sommes tous sauvages"

WITH THE SUN IN LEO

two winds vied so a new storm
jammed in under the old

white-cliffed thunderheads heaved by with evening
& then trailing the last of the west smaller ships

the girls that night stole our towels as we sat
ladelling water spiced with cinnamon & cloves onto the

sauna's hot coals so naked we had to snatch them
down from the rafters while they laughed &

for this they were thrown to the waters
where they lay composing new constellations

& picking out their adopted star in Lyra
while high above the cabin Cygnus

sailed on Arab names through the desert galaxy
Deneb Gienah Sadr Albireo

and the Little Dipper with its precious handle-tip
stood on the studded surface of the lake

THE WATER

the water has not moved
i have moved the water

i lie with my head over the side
waiting for the sun to flood me

under my lids i go blood red
the sun is this blood

the raft rocks in a small wind
i shiver and my eyes

pale to pink to orange to yellow
and i stare it to green to blue and

i am ready   it clears to white glare
the sun cuts the glare

and out i fall into my open eyes
blinded and ready   my head first

into the cool waters of the lake
i push out air from my lungs

I gasp

EPICENTER

(i)

by the waterlilies two small noses making arrows
then nothing

day bakes through and drops sky
into the middle of the lake

a catspaw leaps the pines & pats a black hole
in the blue

circles take off after each other never catching
till they pile up at the edge

there is brief calm at the center and marsha says
if you are jewish you have no place to go back to

(ii)

my eyes fix on the epicenter till
other ripples scratch it out

I walk down to the boat   a fish rises
leaving its own circle from hidden lips

my eye is caught in the brush
by the salt-lick

i quiet to a rock   our circles meet and waver
a pair of ears flick in my direction

i stare   and my eyes go out

she has gone back to green without a ripple

17

A WATERLILY FOR YOU

in that minnesota lake it pulled evening
around it

deep in its yellow
insects feasted like bedouin chiefs
at an oasis

in its cool heart just sweet succulent
coolness

i had seen it from the cabin the only white
among yellows

i rowed out & picked it

i dipped it into the lake

the lake came out cooler

NORTHERN LIGHTS

Mars a red column in the north lake
& taking its sky a steel glow

loosening to ice-flares before our eyes almost
too taut to catch them

& then grinding to a fall while
we sat still watching

till a loon called & an owl & we
turned to the western sky where Venus lodged

in a blue pillar waving over the world
thin silk in galactic winds &

an arm sailed out to anchor
in the east

then faded to a clue while we stood closer
awaiting its return and our release

*

moving up the creek from the south
the half-moon warmed our eyes
& the stream was gold
coming at us slowly through the reeds

SAUNA

no escaping this—
rocks spit & steam as it hits
shudders us out of our skins
as if someone were walking on our grave

our secret is open
lake-water rarefied with herbs
pushes us to the limit
& beyond
so the heart bangs in our ears
as it did for the first Ojibwa
carrying in hot coals with forked sticks
knowing Mide Manitou
patient for the killing and return

                    *

in the dark our pores widen to one another
adolescents & adults male & female
so flesh, dark as new
reaches out & out to

then i rush & stumble down steps
smash the moon
& draw up all silk onto the raft
waiting for a word a touch
with lungs so deep they fill
my whole body

            but
            before i could shout
                    a fish leapt &
                    two white bands in the north
                    stopped the horizon taking on its dark

THE ARRIVAL OF THE COLD

she sits blocking the fire
pulling wet hair to points in her hand
—I teach disturbed children,
  boys mostly, the girls aren't noticed
  in class, they float through school
  and go mad quietly later—

her small square glasses pull her eyes into them
her yellow rubber boots are tucked up under her
she was always cold
& her friend was the only one
she'd take a sauna with
"it's him or nothing"

the kids jibed a little—
what's it like taking a sauna
with a bathing suit on?—

I too felt the difference

                *

so this was the end and the start
I began remembering again
I was ready to come down from the high country

hot resin from the sauna stuck back to shirt
& irritated for the first time
& her playing with a bit of stick
sitting in the hearth
but when she rose and
picking up her torch gathering her cape
went with no farewell
into night into their tent

I noticed the fire and the empty space where she'd sat
and one brand like a torch
burning at one end against the sooty back
and one fly pinging against the glass globes
round the gas-mantles

and I couldn't rise to look again over the lake
or provoke the stars again into gifts
for my eyes   for the night

FINALE

"let be be finale of seem"

one gun and then again   & another

the solitary sandpiper I'd been watching sink
a yellow leg into the creek's jelly
pecking the water & all the while keeping his black eye
beaded on me
he squirted white shit onto a lily-pad &
took off shrilling

I put a foot on the pontoon over a small oil-slick
left by some hunters
who had cut their way through last fall
& shot holes in the floats

                    & another

just when I'd crossed and begun to see deer spoor all over the path
they'd taken for their own
some fresh & runny & some
close to the cabin & when
leaving clockwise
I was about to walk off the path
into close brush where deer fattened for winter
buttoning to the new cold of late august
that threatened continually
to drug me to sleep under the red pines

                    & another

I lay back on needles pulling up my collar
my bowels moved & the sun bled white
I was ready to go

                                    & another

& another—
            this time the cabin door slamming across the lake

turning
I noticed the white spruce I'd stood up
that first day had fallen over again
so I wedged it like a dead viking on its feet
& lay down covering my face with my hands
among second-growth trees on cut-over land
while off round the point trees rubbed together
with chainsaw rasp

I lay back   opened my eyes under closed lids
to bitumen green-veined black
& lifted my palms   a yellow seeped in
& then opened my fingers allowing my eyes through

dead twigs rose to pine-tufts

                            *

above the creek
a great blue heron sailed its long neck
into the lake's dull glass

                            24

RAY'S PLACE

for RB

FACES

green faces have parted the ferns
the sumac has trembled as from a bite
all night
locked in the window while the gale
batted stars about like ducks
the heart kicked in its bed
till the faces called to it
and strode it
balanced like a spear
from beneath three blankets
over quartz and granite
over stumps smouldering with decay
acute
attic
tough as snow soon to be born
from stars filling the window
with clear faces

REACHING

The rock has locked itself away
Though red flags droop from sticks & red blazes slash trunks

Water has become the path
From a fashion for footholds a slow dripping upward

At the final haul up the scree the rock rots
Into dominoes sliding at your fingerholds

Aboriginal mud at the rock's heart loosens in this late spring
Snow flurries settle on it and drift inward

At the top spruce close as kelp mask the drop
To the quarry and its deep water fresh with no outlet

Water silks down the rockface even in summer through
Heavy moss bright as cat eyes holding the face together

Under a bluestone plate at the crumbling wall-foot
Three white eggs like pin-mould or dice-dots

From here a bird's flight dips to the corners
Of the landscape away from dog-howls at noon or valley-roar

There are holds on the land the land lessens with its distance

At its furthest point it reaches itself

Eyes strain to reach it reaching itself

MOUNTAIN REVENGE

The harp called down waters
The water called down mountains
From high loose boulders
A blade of grass called down vengeance

From the heart of the dustcloud
Heat stifling as hands
The harp insists
It has brought nothing but confusion

The heat has all departed in a herd
Women have laid down their rakes
The summer pasture closes at the stream
Flowers call in their exhausted colors

A sound stiffens the falling water
It is nothing
It is the land moving away from the shore
Moving in on itself

Grit clicks in the crops of fowls
Eggs fall in the straw
What hatches is not
The egg's core

But night with yolk still on its head
Closes the shell behind
It has made nests in hollow peaks
Tomorrow the mountain will hatch

THE FLY

they are at bay
tearing down the remaining air
they have failed to kindle it

as I watch
they fumble their flights
trying to strike some life back
into their feet whose tongues
manage to shoot messages
in a dance over the new suns
and into the northern dark
outside my window with its coarse netting

old flies join them from old lairs
for this room is well known
and the garden is an empty crater
hung with dry wind-stalks

Here is the room for last flies
bringing down paint-scales
and from rafters rat-bane
Here the Fly can hear
his own off-gold voice
career again between the many images
of his own hundred eyes
and pierce spaces
I had only thought of cleansing

WINTER LINES

the black balloon
that raises no appetites
but sits
pushing out our sides
nagging us to that air
to that echo of light
luminously black
till we see it pushing through our pores
like mist
forming and reforming all about us
till we are trapped
and cannot cut our way out
and are too heavy to rise
too bleak to flower
the inside of a tumulus

waiting for some breach
some sun-slit to carve
this black flesh we are forced
to see through
our breathing is our voice
and we breathe to each other
in ferns frosting the inside
despair in false flowers and stalks
waiting for the sun that never seems to come

the garden has slid down
and melted on the floor
we will have to talk now
in puffs and grimaces
till the air grows huge
the caul thins
and where we burst
dogs are licking the moon
burning their tongues on its ice

the moon is floating from our navels
the sky is full of moons
swimming in each other's shadow

they are silver and gold
the night is purple between stars
voices that thread night
gather into one shawl
the globe of each in each
and when they talk together
the body whispers in its broken night
calling them in to identify themselves
till they all collapse
rush in on one another
in on the body swelling till it laughs
holding in all its hands
the journey and the night's skin
and the scents that have burst on the stars' fingers
and the black balloon crisp as cinnamon
settles on us again
and we sleep

A WALK AT THE WINTER SOLSTICE

*

all the glass
          fills
with light & all the woods are
                    glass

in this turning
time
          I wake
after one night & the house still
groans & clicks

new warmth makes the wood grow flies
                              drop off panes &
                                        creep
from panels and beams

                    one wasp
                        crawls on the floor
                        blackly
                                cricket-like
                                a veteran

With sky scoured summer-blue
the eye needs all its clues
                    the red apple on the table
                    reflecting a snow patch
                    glacial

                         bottles dug from the dump
                         line the window
                                   gather
                         the white glare into them
                         hard to see

*

I start up the trail whose ribs
are cottontail tracks &
snowmobile runners &
                    keep climbing
                    past
                    an owl's wing-tips in
              a snow-fan
                    past
              tree-creepers at a hand's breath
           jumping snake-heads
        sideways & jump
      on to another tree
     keeping the dead alive
                    & then
                          the scramble where ice melts
                          down the quarry face &
                          moss is warm & thrusts
                          against the hand

                    Here are no prints but
                    in the brush-heap by the pond
                    tracks
              stream in to the rabbits' winter-ground
              scat-discs dry on winter feed or
                                      bloodstained

              in a cusp of melted snow

              Here they meet before full moon
              & the snow-crust is stamped out
              as they snuffle against each other & lift
              thin throats
              of anguish

*

feet of one man veering
     to the lip

       halting

then turning back

The ice is mottled with snow-clots
a foot creeks it
the flood
   overlapped
      snow with
fissures of windblown grass
a small pine shouldered
       & allowed back

     *

this is the top
    & now
the stream takes its tower

from the ice-face in the quarry
      loosening snow &
       voicing stones

I walk steeply
    down
      in the bed
      feet of dog & man cross & re-
          cross as I
      plant my boots & kick
         dirt-cloud pebbles cave in
          side crusts

I go by memory for
all marks are masks
features have to locate
my eyes

*

        I let the water
                drop me
                        to the little house & its
                              slope roof &
                                    Dutch doors &

flies whose blood
darkening by the minute
washes into wings
courses down capillaries in
black bellies sluices
round a million eyes boring
windows and peering into the
widening pores of old wood

*

On the attic window snow has melted to flowers
through it the moon
                  succulent as spring-water
                            leans
                      onto the snow
                        traces blueness to
                              its source &
                      laps it up like
                  skimmed milk
                slides

silk over the snow
                breaks an outcrop
                      snags briefly
                            on bleak grass and weed

CAT WINTER

i

cats in boneless snow
what world will you save tonight

ii

fish of air in the stream
slip under ice
cats' eyes follow starlike
smash the crust with one glare
flip the stream on its back
covering the whole sky
with jack-knives and scales

iii

on this land-spur
I am looking for land
bats of my house
brothers of the same pod

iv

Lord I try to keep warm
guarding the glass I plucked from the fire

I walk through mined landscapes
where cats have made palaces
of catastrophe and cataclysm

their breath is flutes whose teeth
make walls leap
the air is light

v

cats have bitten the glass
making its white fire wholler
I sit by the quiet window
watching them tear tired colors
from the one lamp
lush before with peonies and roses
where birds had perched till fall
till they swallowed the knives at their throats

it is beginning time

vi

now birdbeaks sing in ice
a sharper music
of deadness' finesse
sharp lines' vivid wealth
bleeding that makes the heartier ghost

striking the mind to remember

vii

cats when you sleep tonight
nothing can loosen the stars

TRACING

(i) The Purchase

the stream's storm-memory pitching
past the dutch-door and red pine

*

a child's call
mamma

*

twenty and
fir-straight
four legitimate children to the smith
forty and
russian jewish catholic unitarian
filling boxes losing her humor
to capitalists wars jews &
for her late spring in winter
this undue child
mamma

*

the floor trembles like moss
nails through the roof star-points
   sparks welded to the child eyes
   drawing blood from his eyes
   the magnet drawing steel from the egg
   of his eyes
   mamma

*

hunters' fires have fused
schist and bottle

he has collected them
and placed them in the window

light keeps them alive &

his eye caresses colors for their names

one good eye tries nailing down
all that lives in unfathered
free space
naming what it has never seen before
buying his first land for a
mountain of being
flying dogtag for inner and outer eye
quester eye making the skeleton solid
while as he walks in his woods
whole threads of ear begin to weave
an unseen world untouched
with colors of no color
& beauty wild to run over all
as if it were fire and print
the color from within over all
the changing surface
makes a continuous net catching
the very quality of the dark so that when each of his senses
has the form of its own particular emptiness
the world begins to fill and the overflow
plunges past the half-open door

*

the stars have left the forest
and crawled into the cellar
the bounce in the floor has stopped

   once again he can hear
   as in a tree-top's whisper
   the blood's migration of color
   the russian grainmaster his grandfather
   seeing his daughter's veins and eyes
   in a strange land
   selling the german blacksmith
   a girl of eighteen
   to shape

mamma

   twenty years beating
   till she left

   books and meetings and the little church
   politics of the flesh and spirit

   an irish priest he never knew
   to call

father

          *

what does your father do?
what's his name?

which child could say
I am a child of love?

          *

44

who dared call him liar?

*

gouts strung from trees

fly-wings in webs
bodies' shells in the window-corner and the wind
shaking them all some
free in a wild spiral inside the room
further than the wind
further than the lumbering hill
birches' silver lodes turning the quarry
on its head the bullfrog
leaving darkness different than he found it

*

the bluestone is slicked by hollyhocks
and nettle
the high whine of the nerves
the heart's repeat
the call of a grown man in a church
the echo
the stone steadying
for the new owner of this tract
fathering his own land past the
young priest with no name
in the city of no name

*

you are a child of love

and his insides hear
  of rape and force and rape

he sees the slum and convinces himself
of a happy childhood

he makes the silent mother
happy
   mamma

*

mullein has turned to seed
goldenrods try to shake free
their yellow caterpillars as they rot
st. johnswort has turned at last
pagan petal to air
and in the fir recedes
his own first marriage twice consummated
the two year cancer of belly and genital
his daughter disappeared
death rape love bleed
into the stream
past the door

*

no one here all winter
when air is ice and buried in their bite
lie horsefly and mosquito

*

from the mountain across the valley
the light has opened wider
floats in heavy above the rain
with a scenario of pine and swallows
to dance bat and lion
from the bells of woods

dropping where the road might be
and young pinoaks hustle the slopes
younger cypresses cool the burnt land

*

the trees have started their own breeze
spraying birds like pollen into
spontaneous air

hath the wind a father

noon jostles past
well-joisted
its corners fitted to a knife-blade

sky's grain so close
blue itself could not slip between

the rain has made mirrors
eyes with no backs

the forge fathered
the father forged

light becomes familiar
as the brook discovered in each storm

*

children with no fathers
swing on ryegrass and thistle

(ii) The Delirium

a shuffle of wind and a star
red enough to burn flaps
just under the skin
where the skull aches through
the face's mask and in the nose
groans and creaks dry as cedar
on a bluestone scree
thumbs behind the eyes scraping
bark and face—joints blinder
than a cotton-winged grasshopper
springing from beneath a dark sole
teeth eased from the jaw
and the star amanita soaking up the sky
filling the window from the right corner
to nearest the eye glaring
leaving the head shrunken boneless
brain strung through the nose
sockets collapsed into cowries a skin
parched as the dead cricket on the sill
clicking in the dead wind
shorting night and silent morning
shivers the broken lampshade
moths collapsing into the afterimage
keeping the sky off

*

in the wood's burnt over clearing
a child is tracing his head
on the blue rock

RAY'S PLACE

Nails have been driven through the roof
Their points shine
into the house for tall people

A straw hat on the wall moves the wall outward
The window high as a clerestory
brings the trees inside

Cut in the roof a choice of night
where the sky's dark forest
balances pinwheels as buds

At dawn well water's drunk slowly
and the glass held against the window
drains the land to the mountaintop

THE HAND OF THE HILLS

for Countess Karolyi

A HAIR OF THE DOG

The tail of the dog
sits in the sun
It has not seen the dog
for some time
let alone the sun
The tail is sitting on the dog

I have lain here drawing
not the tail or his dog
but the water-slick of fig-leaves
on the lace curtain
over the door
and more especially
the light that escaped
that slipped the leaves
inundating coasts and fjords

Somewhere between light and shadow
falls a shade
and in that shade
more light than ever fell

I turn and regard something
definite—
from blood on the white walls
to wings shapes still while bodies
are scrim

and end with webs' catscradles
when the light drops
from atop
and the eye is sideways

Somewhere behind a tail is
wagging itself
If I could find the tail
If I could interrogate the dog
If I could move the sun
and its coat of hairs

THE HAND OF THE HILLS

"O my mother!"   I call you
with my hands like a snout
about my face. There is
a ploughshare above the door
and windows are barred to the hillside.
But inside there are
lamb-fat candles and a hearth
where chestnuts used to burst
like hot brains.
I walk across the heights
of spear grass, and my voice cuts
across the valley, and the white
doves wheel baffled at the echoes,
mother.

I put my mouth to the underwater
shadows of insects, haloed
on the flat rock.   I look
down the waterfalls into
oilblue ombrage, and I call
to no end: where we had to squeeze
that weed into the water,
and below, the demon-father
scooped them up, drugged lives:
where the grenade would explode,
and we had to collect purple bodies,
mother.

But the house was ours:
I call down the grey steps
into the ruined parterre, burst
a cherry, a snake burst
under my feet, in the cool corner
by the dead fountain. A whole

copse in the garden I could
not control. The house
rises up like a giant
bluff. The red roof
is like a layer of liver.
I ask where you are, but
there is no water in the pool,
mother.

There is a brown snake
under the terrace that eats
pine martens and some
of our chickens; an old man
snake who's taken over
the porch. I walk over him
every morning, as if
he were a piece of charred
rope. The sheep have packed
dung hard as bitumen in their
fold. They were not milked
as they should have been. They
were driven down to the valley
when the sun burnt
the nails on my hands. But
inside the house, mother,
unused pans are cool,
wooden ladles unused
to hands, ashes in the chimney-
piece grey as dead faces,
and the powderhorn is empty.
It is all as you left it, but
the broom flower is crinkled
like a dead ear. If you come back
we can pick more. I clasp

my hands again around
my mouth and call, as I call
the sheep, clear and mournful.
Why won't you hear,
"mother!"

Far off, at the side of a
lava flow, among the broom
and paper-winged blue
butterflies, a ewe, heavy-withered,
lifts her head. Her mouth
is green, gat-toothed.
Her wool is like a well-trodden
carpet, lighter than the smooth
grey rock she clips over with her
button-black hoofs, snuffing
the air for the voice, and breaks
brusquely into the oak-scrub and
burnished broom, on the pebbled path
down to the springs and the stream.
Her old udders dryer than the rock
the pubic moss dries on. She
bends and sucks the water as from
a teat, watching through the ripples
her ordinary eyes. She lifts
her head at the voice,
dribbling from between
yellow teeth. She lifts
her head, breaking the water
with a forehoof, wrung-withers
tense and thoughtful.
It is her son she hears
above, on the bluff.
"mother!"

There is no flock to consider,
no shepherd. She roams as she
roamed in the other years,
free, lonely as memories,
nibbling delicately
on wild artichoke, scrub,
the grass like burnt hair,
distending her stomach
on spring water. Her son's
voice was not as she remembered.
She bleats.
He hears,
crashing down the slope
like an avalanche,
gourd-clenched balls
swinging tightly. His
horns butt the wind,
dust settles on leaves.
He sees her and stops,
balls swinging slowly, like
bells.

        "Mother,
so often I called,
there was nothing to hear,
all echoes of myself. You
have been where I never heard,
among streambeds and bushes
sound could not reach: you
have been as one dead. You
must come back. My father
still lives under the terrace,
an old bullwhip living
on rats, gnawing his own
stomach, under the ploughshare."

She looked at his tense wool
of summer, flanks like a house,
belly like standing timber,
balls heavy as grenades. And she turned
her sheep's head to the hills,
where the roof tottered
in haze, and to the sheepfold and
ampitheater of hills closing
like a hand; dropped her head.

"If I come I will get lost
in the rooms, fear the blood
in the earth, on the ploughshare.
I will scrub pans till holes show through,
and you will consign me to a room
under open rafters
where spiders hang."

"Never! The garden is yours,
to make the fountain flow again.
Cherries fall like aches and rot
in the grass. Wild strawberries decay
like eyes where you replanted them,
and pigeons wilt like melted wax.
All is yours: the past has gone
like winds to haunt the heavens. Come,
mother, make the old house
a place to live in, where we used
to live, where I have stayed, and called
to you each night and morning."

She looked at the red roof: white
wings sputtered and gutted in the late
red of evening. A dog barked
like a stone falling. A wind

59

shrivelled her fleece. And she looked
down the muted hillside to the
sounds of the stream and crickets.

"If I come you will not sleep
at nights—"
                "Sleep at nights!
I sleep gazing at the holes in the roof,
at the dark wash of the sky
and colter-points of stars!"

"You will sleep less, and nothing
will change. I will knock
into furniture and tread ashes
into the floor: bang in the woodyard
at night, leave doors open:
toss on my knees in the soft
bed. A house is no
place for me any longer.
I have to watch myself, what
I am or may be, now you are
able," she paused, "and your father
dead.
        I sleep on gorse, and drink
when I want to; have all
day to atone, and all night
to weep, if I want to. You must
look to your house, and the liver-
colored roof, and the white pigeons,
and your flock. I've forgotten
how to live in houses.
Goodbye.
Call no more,
my son."

She turned back to the pools,
and the dark lights of the water,
and the soft green lips of the moss,
without turning to watch him
climb back into
the hand
of the hills.

A DIALOG OF DISTANCES

i

you are on a far shore

your mother in her
nostalgia for survival
picks at your voice
under her waist

my poverty   my child

on a blank shore
I thought I heard a creak like silk

I wear you
a thick girdle
elbowing my sides

the cask of your voice
is a language I have never pried
but I am trying to pick
then somehow I shall crawl in with you
and we can sit across from each other
two lengths of silence

ii

I hear you

I am here like a weight
round the heart
dischords of bells and the crash
that hurls your voice
far from itself
over tawny gorges

away from the shore that curls
in on itself like a hair

I will have to be plucked out
I have been growing here far too long

you would be amazed at me

iii

my linen dress
is beginning to fade

how long must I count
the term of your coming?

iv

I am a ball of silk
always unwinding

if you follow
there is no rest

the king of the mountains
has my voice
and you
have my insect heart
that beats on thistle and broom
through the race of summer

this little heart can never give up
for all your pursuit

NORTHERN GARLAND

for Basil Bunting

NORTHERN GARLAND*

Uccelli che parlate il mio dialetto.
—*Andrea Zanzotto*

The spuggies are fledged
some time back &
fluff their feathers on stangs
like old clouts

The mason whose whetstone you can hear
is Bercilac's brother
On the canopied parchment of this valley
ths snow snitters full snart
The warbeland wind wapps
from the heights
& Bloodax dies in this crumpled
paper landscape
gills & burns pressed in
with the edges of fingernails
then trace
May on the bull's side

The fells are gripped in lark song
The bull is more than beef
love more than convenience
The yold-ring chirrups anent
the rown-tree and the keek
of small frogs keeps what cannot move
in hands keened with frost
as the shepherd calls "Iska!" through
then thrusts them flat in this oxtar

The bull is best far off

---

* For a glossary, see last three pages

67

His heraldry I kep in his speech:
"it was sitten on its hunkers
howkin glinters fra amang the het ass
when the lowe tench its claes
and brent it to the verry arse"

Such bulls are worth earthquakes
In the vetrified shining scoria
his horns are twin peaks
his scorched hide
the southron and the city's doom

                    *

Kelds on the Coquet slip loosely
carrying the steg's shadow gray as
slate skimming from a high scout
Thin as a scale-dish the monument
gans with the brabblement of the moment
then shutters again
brattles braying images and water

In such time I brian the oven
with more white paper
amid batts that blow with grass
shugged off high bents where ewes
in boughts yowk to be milked
give what is made & make relief
in the time created
between layking and labbering
that time more than distance
when the will flows against itself
& desires what it needs but
does not want
as Gawain draws near the stiddy

& would not return home if he could
for the stiddy is a beeld
of his own hands
a brat that holds greening
fog of the scree
the wind-harrow's turned
to a shackle-bane that tests
& nicks the fozy neck
& sends him home to the sea

*

The gifts on my nails are whiter
than the gowl in my eyes
If I press my tips together
so the gifts gleek with whole white
it is steadying visions in crags
& not in clarts
I stare and remember hard things
though my claggy feet plodge
While I greet over live guests
there are statues in the crags

*

So heart-scad ower the heugh
gans the hobthrust of my holm
I can howk my howl-kite &
bear a live bull pissing four
red streams
No chance of his being but
a spelk in the eye's gowk
the gimmer who is what you make her
a mere gliff into the gowpen:
open & there are rafters & steeples

The gray-stones dragging in darkness
as words fail the mason's chisel
are stonechats remembered then seen
sitting on his hide at sundown

*

I hoy at the fade this Cheviot bull
though manytime he was scumfished
with the burnt bannock I tossed him
young craw no guts in my brain
& though I worked bulls in clarts
or picked at them with an ice-shoggle
from no high fells no scars nor
scouts rigged and furred
like the riggin of no house I have known

This fit I geek with my guts
With the blood-ax
slit the belly-rim and on the bowk
of the slaughter-oak chisel letters
before the pash

*

Now the bull steams
an illumination on the page
that stretches far as Lindisfarne
& which the lark has opened
to the mason's mallet
tapping on the hide studs of bright brass
He chisels brightness on the shield
so amputated years will know this sign
& dung not soil the mosaic
motif of Northumbria

*

The spuggy perches
on the silver crescent
on the piper's sleeve
The spuggies canny bairns
are gowdin on the inkhorn

FLOATING

On his back
deep cold scoring his spine
the wind from scarred headlands
crushes thyme
coats him in resin
Rock reptile skin claims him while a dove
in the gale beats backward to haven on an eyeball
Skin between his toes quickens his whole body

Arched over the empty orchestra
he tests his temper
provokes the gendering of stones

But turns from black water
follows warmth soft as a camel foot
Till the smell flares his nostrils out

Clambering over dark rocks
face to cave's warm thigh
turning
a man form white as porpoise bone
ankles pierced through water
and where arms should be
nothing

*

Back through mud against the flow
to a stay of tide where cold succumbed
but remained cold

The moment rested till light left the water
and he sought refuge in his bones

                    *

All the sunken cities flared in one fever
and the cry of one seabird
invaded his temple

YEAR OF THE BIRD

Dead scents I couldn't bear bore fruit
and filled earth full of small cuts

Prows split thin ice-gusts
and downwind dropped
opal gardens
spice patches

The birds come
in colter waves
Their wings tatter the straight
They loosen
hot pleats of earth
unfurl them
in loam skies where
harvests wave wide as the sunset
whose winds churn the land
past farmhouse and field
to wild oats and barley
ancestral grasses that
shoulder stones and root

    The birds bring sky in their claws and clay
    Where they settle ears are shaken free
    then cast again in gold
    They have come from nowhere and are going everywhere
    Each place is discovery
    retrieval
    a feather from their breasts

GLOSSARY for "NORTHERN GARLAND"

spuggies: sparrows.

stangs: poles, rails.

clouts: rags.

"the snow snitters" etc., is from *Gawain and the Green Knight* (and so is Ber-cilac). This poem was written in the West Midland dialect of Mercian in the 14th Century. The dialect of "Northern Garland" is, of course, Northumbrian. (Actually, the words are taken from different parts of the county. There is no such thing as *one* Northumbrian dialect.)

gill or *burn:* roughly, synonyms for small valley with stream.

yold-ring: yellow bunting.

anent: in front of, against.

rown-tree: rowan or mountain ash.

keek: peep.

chapped: chilblained.

"Iska!": the shepherd's call to his dog.

oxtar: armpit.

hunkers: to sit on one's heels, to squat.

howkin: digging.

glinters: glowing coals.

lowe: flame.

claes: clothes.

brent: burnt.

keld: oily smoothness on water when the rest is ruffled.

steg: gander.

scout: high rock.

scale-dish: thin dish for skimming milk.

gans: goes.

brabblement: quarrel.

brattle: sound like thunder.

to bray: beat or smash.

to brian: to keep a fire at the mouth of an oven.

batts: flat ground joining islands in a river.

to shug: to swing.

bents: high pastures.

boughts: folds where ewes are brought to be milked.

yowk: itch.
layking: playing.
labbering: struggling like a caught fish.
stiddy: anvil.
beeld: shelter.
brat: film on surface.
fog: autumn grass after hay.
shackle-bane: wrist.
fozy: light and spongy.
gifts: white specks on nails.
gowl: eye mucus.
gleek: deceive.
clarts: mud.
claggy: messy and muddy.
plodge: tramp through water.
greet: cry.
guests: ghosts.
heart-scad: grieved.
heugh: arroyo, dry ravine.
hobthrust: goblin.
holm: island.
howl-kite: belly.
spelk: splinter.
gowk: core.
gimmer: whore.
gliff: glimpse.
gowpen: when one puts fingertips together.
gray-stones: coarse millstones.
hoy: throw.
scumfished: suffocated, choked.
bannock: oat-cake.
ice-shoggle: icicle.
scars: bare and broken places on mountainside.
rigged and furred: ridged and furrowed.

geek: I forget exactly! I think it means 'work.'

belly-rim: membrane encircling intestines.

bowk: trunk, bole.

pash: rain or snow fall.

silver crescent, etc.: emblem borne by Percy's piper—the Percy
   family is the foremost family of Northumberland.

canny bairns: term of endearment.

gowdin: this is what foxes do in the mating season. I have taken
   liberties with the technicality of the term in having spuggies gowd.